CHOOSE LOVE

PEACEMAKERS, PRAYER, AND THE PRESENCE OF GOD IN A DIVIDED WORLD

MICHAEL D. SMITH

First Edition, 2026

ISBN: 978-1-964673-08-0 (Paperback)

Published by Selah Summit Press

Eagan, Minnesota

https://www.SelahSummitPress.com

Cover design and typesetting by Yolandita Colón

Edited by Yolandita Colón

Printed in the United States of America

DEDICATION

I dedicate this writing to my wonderful wife who has been by my side, my partner in serving Jesus. She has encouraged me to go on when I had those moments of wanting to give up. She loved me when I felt unlovable. She called me a "man of God" before I ever was a "man of God! Together, we have raised a family, served in missions, and pursued God's presence. Together we have shared an impossible purpose to see a city changed by an awareness of God's glory.

INTRODUCTION

Dear Friends,

A "defining moment" is the time when a decision is made that shapes destiny. In 1981, God placed a defining vision in my heart—not just to pastor a church, but to pastor a city. That calling has shaped every season of my life and ministry.

Over the years, that vision has grown into a deep burden to see lives restored and communities transformed by the hope of Jesus. I believe we are called to see atmospheres of despair and brokenness turned into atmospheres of hope, healing, and generosity—one life at a time. This has been my prayer for our city, and for my own life.

Psalm 78:71–72 (TPT) says:

"God prepared David and took this gentle shepherd-king and presented him before the people as the one who would love and care for them with integrity, a pure heart, and the anointing to lead Israel, his holy inheritance..."

(with skillful hands — NIV)

Integrity, dignity (honor), humility, and compassion are qualities of effective leadership that reflect the beauty of Jesus. When we lead without these, we create unnecessary conflict and division.

My reputation is how you see me. But integrity is how God—and Sandi, my wife—see me. It's who I am when I'm all alone. When I treat others with dignity—especially those who oppose my opinions and values—and honor those with whom I'm most familiar, it reveals my security in my Savior, not in myself. And when we lack the "skillful hands" necessary to lead, we must depend on the Holy Spirit. Oh, how we need the anointing to lead God's people. Without Him, we can do nothing.

Scripture reminds us of the kind of integrity and example that godly leadership requires:

"Show yourself in all respects to be a model of good works, and in your teaching show integrity, dignity, and sound speech that cannot be condemned, so that an opponent, having nothing evil to say about us, may be put to shame." — Titus 2:7–8 (ESV)

(The Passion Translation paraphrases the latter part: "so that your critics will be embarrassed.")

It is from this vision and burden that *Choose Love* flows.

This book is a compilation of my social media posts, written in response to the everyday issues we all face. In a time of deep division, anger, and confusion, I believe God is calling us—as His people—to live differently:

- To choose love instead of hate
- Mercy instead of bitterness

- Humility instead of pride
- Prayer instead of protest alone
- Healing instead of accusation

My prayer is that as you read these pages, the Holy Spirit will meet you in a very real way—that you will experience His presence, His conviction, His comfort, and His courage to choose love in a culture that often chooses everything else.

I pray that you will experience the presence of the Holy Spirit today—and that together, we will see our homes, our churches, and our cities transformed by the love of Jesus.

With love in Christ,
Pastor Mike
(Michael D. Smith)

CONTENTS

THE 'PRESENCE' STATE

CHAPTER 1

Sometime ago, I read an article on the back story of the sitcom *Happy Days*. It seems that behind the scenes it wasn't always happy. (It was on Facebook so it must be true. Right?) *Jealousy and bitterness* crept in between leading actors over who was getting the most focus and attention. Like most people who must work or live together for a period of time, something happened that brought in separation and division. As a result, when this happens, the joy of friendship can wear off. *The effectiveness of partnership declines.*

This is too indicative of our present societal structure. We all feel the atmosphere of governmental, economic, and familial brokenness and separation. Division is destructive and is often fueled by personal insecurity and an overall lack of confidence. We can't afford to allow the divisions of our current culture to creep into our relationships. We must make every effort to *guard our hearts* from the division that weakens us as a nation and seems to be characteristic of this present age.

Unity strengthens, and according to Jesus, it is highly valued in the Kingdom of God. It produces a strength that can accomplish great things. Healing and joy are the residual consequences. It is so important that we become quick to repent of our own sins and faults, and *quick to forgive* the sins and faults of others. Self-interest, self-promotion, and self-advancement create a lack of "discerning of the body" – in other words, the value of recognizing the need to be one in spirit and in heart.

According to the Bible, this is a cause of why "many are weak and sick among you, and many sleep," i.e., spiritually weak, with a noticeable lack of power. Jesus said: "A house divided will not stand." So, our opposition isn't people, but something even more sinister: a spiritual darkness endeavoring to "steal, kill, and destroy. Its tactic is to introduce the small "little foxes that spoil the vine" into our everyday relationships.

This disunity and division, if it goes unchecked, will ultimately destroy:

- Our joy,
- Our peace,
- Our hope, and
- Our destiny.

Each of us must take time to honestly examine our own heart and attitude before God. When we learn to judge ourselves—rather than constantly judging others—we position ourselves to grow, to change, and to walk in humility. [1]A self-examined life keeps us open to God's correction and protects us from unnecessary judgment.

LED BY THE SPIRIT, NOT BY EMOTIONS

We live in *emotional times.* Emotions can be wonderful. But the problem lies in always being led by feelings. We become susceptible to making wrong decisions that affect our future and our relationships when our emotions are high. Emotion-led people seem to always *react* to the outward, surface circumstances that are always prevalent. They can become angry, frustrated, and bitter—and they tend to become depressed when things don't go the way they plan. Rather than being in control, *they are controlled* by their surroundings.

But you were meant for so much more. You were meant to be led by something far more life-giving and hopeful. "Those who are *led by the Spirit* are the sons and daughters of God,"[2] the Bible says. As we mature, we begin to see things from a higher perspective. We don't judge "after the flesh." You don't rush to judgment. Jesus said, "Stop judging by mere appearances, but instead judge correctly."[3]

> *"So we have stopped evaluating others from a human point of view. At one time, we even thought of Christ merely from a human point of view. How differently we know Him now!"* (2 Corinthians 5:16, NLT)

We must see others the way God sees them, rather

than see them from a natural and emotional point of view. This means valuing people from heaven's perspective—not by natural sight or emotional reactions when we feel offended. We must see others as *the focus of God's love*—even those who ardently oppose us and resist His love. God loves even the most unlovable. He loves you and me. When those whom others previously thought of with contempt have an encounter with Jesus, we want to be the first person they would think to call. Therefore, we must position our hearts to love them and pray for them more than we judge them—especially right now.

We can't afford to have a heart filled with *bitterness*, nor can we afford to hold onto an emotional, judgmental attitude. Instead, pray first—and who knows what God might do?

THE PRECARIOUS STATE

What if we were the solution to the complex problems facing our "precarious state"?[4] Yes, it is too easy just to point our finger at failed government policies. But what if, instead of fixing the blame on faulty decisions made, we would realize that maybe we are called to "fix the problem"? Maybe we are the ones who: "Have come to the city and state for such a time as this!" What if we demonstrated mercy so much more than we show judgment? What if we would "spend ourselves on the hungry" and "help the oppressed in the time of trouble"?

If we did—and this would call for a significant change in our thinking—we have this promise from Isaiah: We are called to be a restorative people. We are the ones who will "build the old waste places" and "raise up the foundations of many generations." Our legacy will be a name of healing—"Repairer of the Breach, Restorer of Streets to Dwell In." In modern terms, this is our charge: to "restore old ruins, rebuild and renovate, make the community livable again." This is more than ancient prophecy; it is our present job description. [5]This calls for an unprecedented humility leading to an unprecedented unity.

I admit that I don't have the full strategy at this moment, other than to replace "malicious talk" with prayer and the "pointing of the finger" in judgment with extending our hands in mercy. We must cry out to God on behalf of Minnesota. Then we must release systemic generosity to break systemic poverty. (See Isaiah 58:6–12.) Could it be that when we awaken to our common mission of being the solution to restore our city, then we will see what God can do?

> "*Let the priests, who minister in the Lord's presence, Stand and weep between the entry room to the temple and the altar. Let them pray, 'Spare your people, Lord! Don't let your special possession become an object of mockery...'*" (Joel 2:17)

Could this be the time we gather together and weep and cry out for mercy until the "Precarious State" becomes known as "**the Presence State**"?

> "*And the name of the city from that time on will be: 'The Lord is there.'*" (Ezekiel 48:35)

We all desire that throughout our nation this would be the identity of Minnesota and our city. There is a change coming. When the foundations are being destroyed, what can we do? It seems like the solid foundations of a once healthy nation are crumbling. There seems to be an effort to ***redefine*** what once was basic life. For some:

- Marriage has been redefined,
- Family structures have been redefined,
- What is male and female has been redefined,
- Morality has been redefined,
- *Integrity* and ethics have been redefined,
- Even what is *appropriate language* has been redefined.

The word "foundation" is defined as: "An underlying basis or principle. The natural or prepared ground or base on which some structure rests. The basis of anything: the moral foundation of both society and religion."[6] Psalm 11:3 says, "When the foundations are being destroyed, what can the righteous do?" The first and most important thing we must do is *pray*. Never forget that "prayer changes things."

Secondly, we must **take action** to demonstrate the reality of the power and presence of the love of God. Never forget that one encounter of His love through you is a force from heaven that can change the hearts of humanity. You may feel like your whole world is falling apart. Be assured that:

- God knows you,
- He is for you,
- *He cares about you, And He will never fail!*

So when you feel like running away—run to God. Never give up on hope—expectation is the groundwork for miracles.

> *"And this hope will not lead to disappointment. For we know how dearly God loves us, because he has given us the Holy Spirit to fill our hearts with his love."* (Romans 5:5, NLT)

THANKSGIVING, BLESSING, AND THE ATMOSPHERE AROUND US

CHAPTER 2

I love Minnesota, and I love the Twin Cities. So, when, in recent times, with struggles and problems that seem so great and *unsolvable*, I find myself grieved in my heart. It tends to be our natural reaction to those problems to burst out with judgment, and there has been reason to complain.

Lately, there has even been an increase of our leaders, in anger, using vulgarity and cursing in public. It has had an effect on the atmosphere. Everyone can physically feel it. It seems to go right through you. And it doesn't produce hope. Just anger and more despair. However, *I am convinced that there is another way* – a better way of responding.

It is having a lifestyle of *giving thanks*. This becomes a sacrifice when it replaces an emotional desire to grumble. In the middle of the difficulties and lack, it actually becomes prophetic. Instead of just seeing the apparent problems, it looks ahead to see the *potential promises*. It looks ahead to see what God will do to bring out His purposes for Minnesota. I believe that *blessing* is so much more powerful. That is why I am convinced that God's people, releasing daily blessings, speaking blessing, and being thankful, will have a *greater effect* on the environment of our neighborhoods and our state.

People are drawn to those who see the potential in the middle of the problems. They are drawn to those who have peace in the middle of the storm. They are drawn to those who see the healing presence of Jesus in the middle of the hurt. In the middle of loss and brokenness, a thankful person will begin to see there is purpose. In the middle of the struggle, a thankful person will have an expectation for the promise. And when it looks like you've been forgotten by God, your choice to remain thankful will open your eyes to His presence—and you'll realize He was there all along.

The reality is—sometimes it is so difficult to be thankful. But when gratitude becomes a *lifestyle*, it transforms your way of life. When you become contagious with appreciation for the littlest things, you will become an agent of change in others. I am thankful that you are that person.

"We are the champions..."

When we hear that, we think of sports heroes like the leading scorer of the Timberwolves, or the number one golfer in the world. We often define a champion as one who wins, a victor, a hero, or a superstar. But they can also be defined as one who supports another, an advocate, or one who defends. No matter how you define it, *it requires a high price to be a champion*. There is a cost to be in this category. It really takes laying down your life. If you want to be excellent in whatever you do, it *necessitates personal suffering* to be of more value than personal comfort.

Really, there are so many *unknown* champions in this world. They're often seen as ordinary, everyday people—never drawing attention to themselves, yet crucial to the life and support of others. They are the nurses, the caregivers in senior centers. Those who faithfully serve the homeless. The teachers who go the extra mile. The neighbors who watch over their fellow neighbors. The young men and women who willingly go into battle to *secure freedom and hope* for many.

In times past, when civilizations were in spiritual darkness, the Bible says that when people cried out to the Lord, He would send them champions, governmental and spiritual, who would give their lives to take up the cause to bring healing to the land. We so need these kinds of champions again.

There is a distance between *excellence and mediocre*. It is often called "just good enough." It is where many are content to live their lives, satisfied with just getting by. It is comfortable. It doesn't cost anything. There is no price to pay for this lifestyle. But rarely, if ever, does this describe a *champion*. When there is no cross to carry, there is no understanding of a real "joy set before you." It requires a high price to be a champion.

Jesus is the ultimate Champion of all humanity.

"Jesus paid it all,
All to Him I owe.

Sin had left a crimson stain,
He washed it white as snow."[1]

You know, Memorial Day is a day of honoring. We **honor** all who gave their lives, who paid the ultimate price in securing the freedoms we hold on to. *But honor as a lifestyle is a mark of a functional civilization.* To honor others is probably one of the most overlooked values that impacts life. The truth is, the more you give and give voice to honoring others, it creates a life-giving, core strength in your own life. True success in relationships (family, business, etc.) are the lasting results. The more you intentionally honor others, the *more potential* you have for an abundant, "long life" and for things to go well with you.

The opposite is also true. The more we hold on to attitudes that seem to be given to always criticize and even despise others, it complicates and spawns conflicts in your own relationships. The fruit of this is that things will not go well for you, and you spend your life *always struggling to survive*, never experiencing the peace and joy that God intended for you to have. True wholeness is found in embracing *a lifestyle of honor*, forgiveness, being merciful, and holding on to what – and who – is true.

"*Be devoted to one another in love. Honor one another above yourselves.*" (Romans 12:10, NIV)

PEACEMAKERS IN A CULTURE OF CONFLICT

CHAPTER 3

There is a great need today for *peacemakers.* We have way too many conflict-makers.

Peacemakers are not defined by "the color of their skin but by the content of their character." They are always looking to bring people together. They're always searching for opportunities to bring healing and peace. They become an *influence* that brings unity, wholeness, and healing. They are grieved when there is polarization, *division*, bitterness, and injustice.

They become a sustaining influence on their culture. They're *motivated by forgiveness* and the power of love. Their focus is restoration more than retribution. When others are always trying to expose the flaws of others, they are motivated to "cover over a multitude of sins" because they have a vision for something greater.

Conflict-makers also bring influence—but through intimidation. They often appear angry at those who disagree with them or hold a different viewpoint. They either initiate conflict or keep it going. They tear others down more than they build them up. They believe the only way to find retribution is by exposing faults and flaws—as if that were their mission. And the truth is, apart from God's love, this describes all of us.

By contrast, the sons and daughters of God...

"Are patient and kind. They do not envy, do not boast, are not proud. They do not dishonor others, are not self-seeking, are not easily angered, they keep no record of wrongs. They do not delight in evil but rejoice with the truth. They always protect, always trust, *always hope, always persevere.*" [1]

They never give up!

Are you a conflict-maker—or a peacemaker?

It is only by the grace of God found in Jesus that we can become forgiven and have His heart to release healing and restoration. What will it take to make *real peace* between two warring nations? What is needed to bring *real healing* into our own nation? I am convinced that the single most important thing we can do to *resolve conflict* on any level is to realize how much we need to *forgive* – to refuse to hold on to any offense.

Forgiveness and mercy have the power to heal relationships in our nation, our cities, our churches, and our families. It will save your emotions, your mind, your sanity. It will heal your body and save your marriage. It can save you from financial ruin. There is nothing else quite like it. It might be the most important function of your heart. At the core of every *successful relationship*, between:

- Husband and wife,
- Mother and daughter,
- Father and son,
- Neighbors,
- Even Republicans and Democrats, there is *forgiveness*.

It isn't when we are perfect that we become functional. It is when we are forgiven and when we are quick to forgive. The truth is we all have sinned. "There is no one perfect—no not one." We all need forgiveness, and we all need a Savior. Our greatest need is peace with God, and He longs to forgive us. *Rebellion* keeps us from admitting that we are at fault. *Stubbornness* keeps us from forgiving those who oppose us. But when we submit to Christ and receive and release forgiveness, we become sons and daughters of God—peacemakers.

Jesus taught that division is fatal, declaring,

"*A kingdom divided against itself cannot stand*" (Mark 3:24–25, NIV). Therefore, He pronounced a special blessing on those who fight that division: "*Blessed are the peacemakers...*"(Matthew 5:9, NIV).

If peacemakers are blessed, then the opposite is true: conflict-makers are cursed. Peacemakers do not have the mind of the group; they have the mind of God.

"*You will keep in perfect peace all who trust in you, all whose thoughts are fixed on you!*" (Isaiah 26:3, NLT)

Humility opens the door to forgiveness, which opens the door to unity, which always opens the door to supernatural blessing. (See Psalm 133.)

Oh, how we need peacemakers today.

Be one!

THE POISON OF HATE AND THE ANTIDOTE OF MERCY

CHAPTER 4

Jan-Michael Vincent's chronic alcoholism was a genuine American tragedy. Once the highest-paid actor on network television, at the beginning of his career Vincent looked so good and strong. By the time of his death in 2019 he was an emaciated shell. His body was *slowly poisoned* over the years with *alcohol***.** His life became a nightmarish downward spiral of arrests, fights, drunken brawls, automobile accidents, and incarceration. After decades of absence from public view, Vincent died at age seventy-four, having lost his potential.

There is another form of *poison* that can destroy a person's soul. It is a slow toxicity penetrating our minds. There is something that would try to poison our lives that is so invasive, so undetected. It is *holding onto offense,* becoming *easily offended,* easily embittered, and all too easily becoming condescending to those with whom you disagree. It invades our thoughts unnoticed through the *continual deception and misinformation* that often comes through the opinions of those around us, who are subject to the same *influence* of this current cultural media. It holds us in *captivity*. It always robs us of our destiny and our potential.

Hate is a deep emotional reaction of hostility, usually derived from fear and/or unresolved frustration. It can become contagious based upon shared information that often isn't complete. Therefore, it positions a mind to become vulnerable to deception. Harboring hate results in bitterness and separates a person (in their thoughts) from the grace of God. In our present day, it is so important that we guard our emotions. Deuteronomy 29:29 warns us to, "*Make sure there is no root among you that produces such bitter poison.*"

The only antidote to this spiritual poison is a heart of mercy and forgiveness. This is what breaks the hold of bitterness. It opens up the flow of God's grace in our feelings. Mercy gives birth to more mercy. But bitterness gives birth to more hate. Jesus even said that we are to "love your enemies. Do good to those who hate you." And the more we see the spirit of the antichrist, the more we must express our love for Jesus Christ.

When you do, it will *attract attention*—and produce a more significant change than any unresolved anger. Why would Jesus tell us to "bless those who persecute you and pray for those who spitefully use you"? Why would He tell us to "love your enemies! Do good to those who curse you"? (See Matthew 5:44; Luke 6:27–28)

I believe that it is because He knew that our real enemy isn't hateful, bigoted, ignorant people that we see, *but the spirit of hate,* bitterness, and ignorance that is unseen, all with a purpose to weaken, divide, steal, and destroy. As long as we are constantly focused on the *opposition that we see*, we will react with our own hate and anger, and as a result, the cycle of hate and anger continues.

Whether it is in the nation or in your home, if we are divided, we will fall. (See Matthew 12:25.) When we fight with our own strength and react with our own emotions of hate and anger, we will lose. How many generations will it take us to realize that you can't fight hate with hate? I declare that this is a new season—a new generation. We have come to a place where as a nation we can go forward into healing and restoration, or we can go backward in hate and polarization.

HATE IS THE ENEMY OF HOPE

Hate keeps you bound to the past. Its focus is always reliving past generational hurts (and they are real and painful), and it robs you of future hope. The pain of the past intends to keep us from having a vision of the promise. *"Where there is no vision, people perish"*. Where there is no forgiveness, people are enslaved to the past.

Where there is no mercy, people are bound to judgment. Justified hate and anger reacting to unjustified hate and anger always keeps us in the cycle of hate and anger. There is something far greater than retribution. It is called *restoration*. Hatred will keep us from healing. Somebody must break the cycle. Oh, wait a moment. Somebody did—***Jesus.***

Embracing the cross of Christ will set us free from

hate and anger because Jesus took the judgment of hate on Himself. While the world was living in reaction to evil, Jesus defeated the eternal effects of evil by responding in perfect love.

It might be good to follow Him.

BREAKING THE CYCLE: LOVE THAT WINS

CHAPTER 5

Who will break the *cycle* of hate and accusation? One person will speak against another with anger and contempt, and the other will react harshly with words filled with bitterness and scorn. And the environment becomes filled with vitriol leading to violence. Much of the root of this "poison" comes from having distorted information that fits one's own narrative. Many times, it is with a desire to control, fueled by fear of losing control.

Political group pitted against political group. Leaders pitted against leaders. Sometimes even within family and the church. And hate resulting in more hate. Again, I ask the question: *who will break the cycle*? What can be done to bring change? Who will bring change to the atmosphere over our cities?

Someone needs to stand up and *repent* – to change – and initiate the healing process. In our human nature, we always want the other person, the other group, to be first.

But it might be that it will begin with you and me. I heard my friend William Ford III say, "*The first one to love—wins!*" I want to add:

- The first one to forgive—wins.
- The first one to extend mercy—wins.
- The first one to lay down their life—wins.
- The first one to break from holding to generational offense—wins.
- The first one who will bless instead of curse their enemy—wins.

Because ultimately that is the only way that this thing will turn around. By the way, that is really Jesus' way, isn't it? He offers forgiveness *even before* we repent. He offers the gift of grace even when we don't deserve it. And He loves us even when we don't love Him. This way of responding to our current culture will ultimately usher in the answer to the prayer that has been offered up over and over for ages:

"Thy kingdom come.
Thy will be done
On earth as it is in heaven."
Matthew 6:10, (KJV)

SONS, DAUGHTERS, AND THE FATHER'S LOVE

CHAPTER 6

To be consumed with hate towards anyone is an expression of a *mental dysfunction*. It really demonstrates emotional immaturity. It evaluates everything through the soul, through emotions and feelings, without wisdom and insight. Our level of maturity is found in how we react to others' immaturity and to those with whom we disagree.

The mission of quality leaders is to bring people into *maturity marked by humility.* Mercy and forgiveness is an expression of those who are emotionally mature. We all long for solutions to the problems of broken systems in our hurting humanity. Too many lives have been senselessly taken, all because of latent and unresolved anger, mental illness, and/or rejection.

I believe that much of it is the result of an *"orphan spirit."* This is when many in an entire generation have been confused in their *identity and purpose because of a disconnection with a father's love*. As a result, it seems that in our day "*all creation is groaning.*" (Romans 8:22.) We are groaning.

I believe the solution for the complex dilemma of our day isn't going to be found just in education, politics, and more laws, but found in the hearts of the sons and daughters of God who know *the power of united prayer* and who refuse to stay silent and secluded. They are no longer content with being insulated with just having their own good feelings, but long for fulfilling their destiny to bring restoration and reconciliation to a nation – one person at a time. (See Romans 8:19.)

So, I am convinced that the one thing that is desperately needed is for those who "love God and love their neighbor as themselves" to have *God-given encounters* with a culture that today desperately needs forgiveness, healing, hope, and deliverance from the torment of separation from the Father's love. Our cities need to encounter real love in action. Jesus said: "I will build my church, and the gates of hell will not prevail against it."[1]

In other words, the church that Jesus builds should be *the most powerful influence* in any city or nation. The impact of a face-to-face connection with the reality of the powerful grace and mercy of God will release hope and will change lives profoundly.

> *"Anyone who says, 'I am in the light,' while holding hatred in his heart toward [anyone] is still in the darkness."* (1 John 2:9, TPT)

Becoming Like the Father

He was an imposing figure—six-foot-four. And when he wore his cowboy hat and boots, my dad seemed larger than life. He had a presence about him. I remember when we would walk into a room full of people, it seemed to me as if the whole place would turn and give him attention. I grew up in his shadow—and I loved it. I always felt a sense of security when I was with him.

When I was a child, if there was anything to fear in the darkness of night, being with him would make that fear disappear.

Sometimes, courage comes from being near the presence of strength. When we are with those who are strong, that strength becomes contagious. Courage has the power to transform ordinary people into the extraordinary. That's why the more time you spend with your Father in heaven, the more His nature rubs off on you. He takes what is natural and turns it into something supernatural *(see Acts 4:13).* If there are any qualities most needed in fathers today to be effective, I would rank courage in the top three —along with wisdom and understanding.

- **Wisdom** is to know what to do – the right thing.
- **Understanding** is to know why to do the right thing.
- But **courage** is to do the right thing.

By the way, my father, like yours, wasn't perfect. He developed through the years because he had a willing and *teachable heart.* But he was courageous enough (and humble enough) to change. Most likely, you haven't had a perfect father. But you can become a father (or mother) who will make a difference. Just invest time with your heavenly Father.

He's waiting patiently for you.

CITIES, NATIONS, AND THE PRESENCE OF GOD

CHAPTER 7

Some time ago, as I was standing on the top floor of a tall building overlooking *Ho Chi Minh City,* I heard this question within me: "I wonder who is weeping over this city?" Then I heard the same question directed more towards me:b*"Who is weeping over the Twin Cities?"* The answer today is—we all are.

We weep when our little children are faced with death, crime, and violence in our streets—and even now, at churches and schools. We weep over how the identity of our cities has been tainted in recent years. Do we weep over the *sex trafficking* of our young people? Do we weep over those who are *enslaved* to drug and alcohol addiction, mental illness, and systemic poverty? Do we weep over so many who are *lost without the hope* found in Jesus Christ?

Sometimes it is so easy to disengage from the deep hurt and need and isolate ourselves. We often do this by forming judgments of our city, its leaders, and of those who are caught in the web of darkness. Instead, I believe that we can do something – something we are invited to do by God himself:

> "*Work for the peace and prosperity of the city... pray to the Lord for it, for its welfare will determine your welfare.*" (Jeremiah 29:7, NLT)

We can protest the city in judgment—or we can pray for its peace. Yes, pray. The choice is ours. But I am convinced that when we pray:

- with hearts that are broken and filled with compassion,
- with hearts filled with unprecedented humility,
- with a longing for God-given, unprecedented unity,
- and with the knowledge that we are partners together in purpose,

...then the beauty of Jesus will become evident, and the spiritual atmosphere over our cities will change.

1 Timothy 2:1–8, TPT says,

> "*Most of all, I'm writing to encourage you to pray with gratitude to God. Pray for all men [and children]... with intense passion. And pray for every political leader and representative, so that we would be able to live tranquil, undisturbed lives, as we worship the awe-inspiring God with pure hearts. It is pleasing to our Savior-God to pray for them. Therefore, I encourage the men to pray on every*

> *occasion with hands lifted to God in worship, with clean hearts, free from frustration or strife."*

When Jesus approached Jerusalem (Luke 19:41), the Bible said He wept with "uncontrollable tears" because they had rejected the very thing that could bring them peace—Christ Himself.

Twin Cities, I beg you, don't turn away from Him today.

> "*And the name of the city from that time on will be: 'The Lord is there.'*" (Ezekiel 48:35, NIV)

We desire and pray that from across our nation this would be our identity – that the Twin Cities would be known as: "The Lord Is There."

California's devastating wildfires destroyed roughly 95 percent of Paradise, but one symbol was left standing among the ashes—a cross—giving its residents hope. In the face of such trauma, people are asking, 'Where is the remedy? Where are the answers for those experiencing such devastation, with seemingly nowhere to turn? Is there any hope?'

That solitary cross points to an answer. "*I lift up my eyes to the mountains—where does my help come from? My help [Hope]* [1] *comes from the Lord, the Maker of heaven and earth.*" (Psalm 121:1–2, NIV)

When life for so many seems flooded with *crushing issues* that seem to have no solutions—when overwhelmed with hopelessness, it's in those times that often what is needed most is a change in perspective. It's in those times we need to lift up our eyes from our present despair and set them on our ever-present Savior who is patient and desiring for us to come to Him.

No matter how big, how difficult the problems are, the One who created the mountains is our Creator, and He is our only source of help – the only solution. The only real, lasting hope that I know for the soul that is broken with grief and loss is found in the **cross of Christ.**

Our present experience of shock and anguish is radically changed when we have an encounter with the presence of Jesus.

KINGS, KINGDOMS, AND HUMILITY

CHAPTER 8

No king? What is a king? "The chief or sovereign of a nation; a man invested with supreme authority over a nation, tribe or country; a monarch. Kings are absolute monarchs when they possess the powers of government without control..."[1] At a time when everyone revered Caesar as "lord and savior," when the common culture would declare, "We have no king but Caesar," there came a bishop who defied the cultural norm. His name was Bishop Polycarp, an elderly man who had the distinct privilege of being mentored by the apostle John himself.[2]

All he was asked to do was simply place a pinch of incense on an altar before an image of Caesar. To do so would demonstrate his allegiance to the lordship of the tyrant and spare him the judgment of death. That relatively small gesture would allow him to live. To not do so would guarantee his demise. But he had a conviction that this seemingly minimal act would deny his faith in Jesus.

His famous quote: *"Eighty and six years have I served Christ, and he never did me any injury: how then can I blaspheme my King and my Savior?"*[3] With that, he was persecuted, tortured, and his body burned. In essence, Polycarp said: "I have no King but Jesus."

My question in all of this is: **Do you have a king?** To whom, or to what, have you given *"absolute" control* over your life? What has taken over your every thought? What rules your life? Anger? Bitterness? Stubbornness? Rejection? Misinformation and *deception* have a way of bringing us into allegiance to a false ideology. But "the truth [always] sets you free."

Everybody has a king in their life. I am convinced that the only true King – the only true authority worthy of giving all my life to – is Jesus. I desire to surrender everything to:**"Christ alone."** He alone is:

"The King of kings and Lord of lords—who alone is immortal and who lives in unapproachable light... To Him belong all honor and power, now and forever. Amen."(1 Timothy 6:16; Revelation 19:16)

What would a *"humility flag"* look like? Well first, I don't think humility would fly a flag. But if it did, what would it look like? How does humility differ from pride?

- Pride is condescending. Humility is understanding.
- Pride dishonors others. Humility honors others freely.
- Pride is intolerant. Humility is patient.

- Pride is easily irritated. Humility is easily forgiving.
- Pride criticizes. Humility encourages.
- Pride is self-seeking. Humility is self-surrendering.
- Pride promotes self. Humility promotes others.
- Pride wants to be seen. Humility desires to be hidden.
- Pride is destructive. Humility is constructive. (See Proverbs 16:18.)
- Pride creates conflict. Humility values harmony.
- Pride focuses on others' failures. Humility admits its own failures.
- Pride flaunts its depravity. Humility repents of its depravity.

Sin defined is simply to "miss the mark." And we all have. But rather than always looking at others' sin, if we desire to see healing in our nation, it is imperative that we: "*Humble ourselves and pray* and seek God's face and turn from [our own] offensive ways. Then [God promises that He] will forgive our sin and will heal our land."[4] So... if there were ever a "humility flag," I believe it would contain a cross. Because that is the greatest symbol – the utmost expression of humility that humanity has ever known.

"Pride goes before destruction, a haughty spirit before a fall." (Proverbs 16:18, NIV)

> *"...All of you, clothe yourselves with humility toward one another, because, 'God opposes the proud but shows* ***favor*** *to the humble.'"* (1 Peter 5:5, NIV)

- The proud resist God.
- The humble submit to God.
- The humble desire God.

Some time ago, I had a dream that I was meeting in Washington, D.C. with both President Trump and President Biden—together. I was there to give them this message: *our nation desperately needs healing*. This was the time for them to embrace humility, to put an end to name-calling, blame, and *deception*. This is the time to turn – profound change – to *repent.* I told them this country *needs real, righteous leadership* in policy and personal character. We need someone with a healing voice that recognizes that a "house divided against itself will not stand."

In the dream, they both listened intently *with tears* in their eyes, and stood up, and to my surprise, they held out their arms and *embraced* each other. (I know... it's only a dream.) Then President Biden turned to me and said they wanted to do a photo shoot at my house to remember this day. I knew that I would only have moments to rush home and get the house ready. In the dream, I found *my house in disarray*. A work crew had made a mess of the floors and walls. I was panicking, knowing that the nation's leaders would arrive any moment. In a flurry of activity, we began to sweep debris under the carpet and stuff the closets full of rubble and trash. Then I woke up. In the dark of the night, this word came to me:

> *"If our nation is going to be healed, we need to clean our house first. Cleaning must precede healing. This is not the time to 'sweep anything under the carpet.'"*

We must "clean house" of speaking fear, unforgiveness, bitterness, condescension, and anger directed at those with whom we disagree, more than hope and encouragement with humility. We must not let our differences divide us. We must not let our perspectives separate us. We must extend immediate forgiveness. We will bless instead of blame. **And we must pray.** After all, peacemakers are not "mere men," but they are known as the sons of God. (See 1 Corinthians 3:3.) When we do this, we will be positioned for healing for our nation. Cleaning will lead to healing.

> "*Your love for one another will prove to the world that you are my disciples.*" – Jesus (John 13:35)

JUSTICE, MERCY, AND THE VALUE OF LIFE

CHAPTER 9

"*The great deception*" of a civilization is to not: "Hold as self-evident, that all men are created equal and that they are endowed by their Creator with certain unalienable Rights, that among these are Life, Liberty and the pursuit of Happiness."[1] These words begin the Declaration of Independence. It was in a time when *slavery was an accepted practice almost all over the world* that these words were penned. And even though it was a founding principle on which this country would be established, still many throughout the nation, even to the present day, would continue to suffer from the effects of generations of this pervasive and ugly sin.

Devastated lives and destroyed families have had lasting effects on future generations. *Present-day slavery and human trafficking*, along with *abortion*, have always devalued human life and left many without hope. The only way that mankind could ever justify these atrocities would be to dehumanize humanity and embrace the lie of racism.

At the same time, when *deception is rampant,* we so desperately need to embrace and seek what is the truth. And we need to understand the value of forgiveness. Knowing what the truth is will set us free from the *deception of racism*, and *learning to forgive* will set us free from the bondage of bitterness.Facing our nation's history truthfully—and choosing forgiveness and healing where there's been harm—will shape our future.

This truth is more than just a set of principles; it is a person—**Jesus**. We must know Him personally. And now, more than ever, we must live out the declaration written on our currency: "In God We Trust."

Yet as a nation, we have often drifted from that trust. In 1973, when the Supreme Court ruled on *Roe v. Wade*, establishing abortion as a constitutional right, the decision was codified into law. At the time, few—including myself—fully grasped the far-reaching implications of such a radical ruling. The prevailing mindset was that abortion would be uncommon and rare. We didn't realize that our nation was stepping into a deception that would distort the value of the life of the unborn.

Over time, something tragic happened. There was a gradual shift in the minds of many that has brought about "*abortion on demand*" as a right. Babies became dehumanized, known as only a fetus and an *inconvenience*. As a result, over sixty million babies have been killed, and it is now said, the most dangerous place in our nation became the mother's womb. The place where the very first sound that a baby would hear should be the comforting heartbeat of a mother now became the place where its very *destiny* would potentially be terminated.

Instead of the mindset, "My baby, my responsibility," the current mantra has become, "My body, my choice." The rights of the unborn are often not considered—even up to and through birth. Now, life has been devalued to the point of a national crisis marked by vitriol and violence.

The reality is this: even in the womb, God knows you.

> *"You made all the delicate, inner parts of my body and knit me together in my mother's womb. Thank you for making me so wonderfully complex!... You watched me as I was being formed in utter seclusion, as I was woven together in the dark of the womb. You saw me before I was born. Every day of my life was recorded in your book. Every moment was laid out before a single day had passed..."* (Psalm 139)

I know that the pain of making the decision to abort, and the lasting effects of trauma, have gripped the hearts of many women – and men. But there is good news. *God forgives. He heals hearts. He will restore.* He will wash away the damage of wrong past decisions when we come to Him. So—could this be the time when, if we humble ourselves and repent as a nation, God will hear us, forgive us as a nation, and heal our land? This is my prayer.

I pray for mercy for the unborn—and also mercy for those born without citizenship. You can't have mercy without justice. When one person receives mercy, as a result, someone else will bear the judgment. It is called a "*zero-sum game.*"

Let me explain.

If you show mercy to *criminals* who are here illegally, the ones who will suffer the judgment are those who live where violence and fear are prevalent. The ones who suffer the lack of justice are those who *are human-trafficked or child-trafficked*, and those who are enslaved by the cartel. The ones who suffer are those who, addicted to substances, find that there is now increased access to *fentanyl*, resulting in increased overdose deaths.

Mercy to one will result in judgment – and *a lack of justice* – to another. As a nation, we have to choose. If you make a decision to show mercy towards *biological boys* in order for them to participate in girls' athletics, the girls receive the *lack of justice* of not being able to compete adequately. But if you show mercy to the young girls who have trained most of their lives, limiting the sport only to young girls, *the transgender* person will receive the judgment.

Someone must choose, and someone will be disappointed. Will it be the women, or the men who identify as women? Mercy to one will result in a lack of justice to another. Someone has to choose who it will be. And if you show mercy to demonized terrorists who would even strangle children and babies held as hostages and then even celebrate over their coffins, then *Israel* and the world are held in judgment. Mercy to one will bring a lack of justice to another.

That is our current problem. *Governments were intended to wield justice, and those who would follow Jesus are supposed to show mercy.* When the two are reversed, there is confusion, and we become vulnerable to *brokenness* as a culture. By nature, I am a "mercy-shower." But I must recognize that there is always someone who will receive judgment on the other end. Therefore, it requires *wisdom* to make the right decisions that will maximize future generational integrity and the structural, cultural health needed, that will ultimately result in peace.

> *"He has shown you, O man, what is good; And what does the Lord require of you but to do justly, to love mercy, and to walk humbly with your God?"* (Micah 6:8, NKJV)

Because of mercy, Jesus took our judgment on Himself on the cross – mercy and justice combined.

FORGIVENESS, GENERATIONS, AND HEALING

CHAPTER 10

Do you remember the story of the Hatfields and McCoys? For generations, these two families carried an offense against each other. Hatred took root in their hearts and was passed down to their children and grandchildren, resulting in deep bitterness and ongoing violence.

We too often don't realize how our deep-seated attitudes are "*mental containers*" that can hold on to offense from others. Without even being aware of it, we all are subject to offend, or be offended. When that happens, we often respond by slipping into self-preservation—or we become frustrated, bitter, and angry, sometimes even allowing a *root of bitterness* to take hold.

Our deep-seated ways can even be carried into next generations, keeping the established patterns going. "The sins of the fathers are visited to the next generations." Therefore, our *social conscience* becomes seared and our hearts become hardened. It is in that moment that the only solution is "a broken spirit and a contrite heart." This is what God will actually honor. (Psalm 51.) This alone will bring deep-seated transformation. We so need to be healed of *generational attitudes* that work against hope and build resistance to the healing power of sacrificial love.

- It is when we have *deeply repented* for our own attitudes, even when in our perspective they have been justifiable.
- It is when we have repented of not honoring each other, and repented of not forgiving one another.

It is then that we have a promise:

"Your light will break forth like the dawn, and your healing [of the sickness of hatred] will quickly appear; then your righteousness will go before you, and the glory of the Lord will be your rear guard."

It is then that...

"You will be known as those who restore old ruins, rebuild and renovate, make the community livable again." *(See Isaiah 58, The Message Bible.)*

This is what happens when hearts are truly changed. We all need to be aware and awakened to the condition of our own heart. *Awakening* comes by allowing the Holy Spirit to do a deep work in us—a work that may go further than we previously imagined. Because when we refuse to forgive and withhold mercy—the cycle of pain and hatred just continues. *The beat goes on and on and on.*

She suffered heartbreak after heartbreak. Not only her sons, but also the one who had been her companion, her love, her very heart. Now all gone. No longer among the living. We don't know the details, but that is how tragedy sometimes strikes—premature, unexpected.

And now, living in a foreign land without any apparent support system to sustain her, she turned to her daughters-in-law and told them to also leave her. Make their own way. Start their own life over. But she was at the last of her life and wanted to return to her country where she heard there might at least be some small hope. At least she could die in a familiar environment.

In her grief, she wept and, wanting to separate herself from the pain of her past, she desired to change her name. *No longer Naomi, but now Mara.* No longer "Pleasant," but now "Bitterness." That would be her new identity. And she had every right to be bitter. It seemed that God had forsaken her. I think at times we all have had that thought: "Where are you God? I need you now." But that wasn't the end of the story. God always has a plan. He is always watching over us. Even "when we don't see His hand, we can trust His heart." *Ruth*, her widowed daughter-in-law, said these now famous words:

> *"Don't urge me to leave you or to turn back from you.*
> *Where you go, I will go, and where you stay, I will stay.*
> *Your people will be my people and your God my God..."*
> (Ruth 1:16–17)

Yes, there is more. When we *trust God and are patient*, the narrative will prove to have a beautiful ending. Ruth became remarried to a wealthy, godly man named Boaz. God divinely – and in His time – provided. Not only was

Naomi's identity restored, but in time, she became the grandmother of a little boy.

> *"Then Naomi took the child in her arms and cared for him. The women living there said, 'Naomi has a son!' And they named him Obed. He was the father of Jesse, the father of [the great king]* [1] *David." (Ruth 4:16–*

And generations later, because of God's great love and His great plan, another *Mara*—I mean Mary—*gave birth to the Son of God—Jesus.* Just think—Naomi could have possibly ended the succession of Christ in her family line *if she gave into her bitterness* because of her loss. But instead, she went from *Mara* to Mary. From "Bitterness" to "Beloved."

Sometimes you just have to let go, and let God!

PRAYER, PASSION, AND A HIGHER PERSPECTIVE

CHAPTER 11

Just recently, several million people across the nation gathered together to protest. They weren't motivated to come by a desire to hear a specific speaker or their favorite musicians. They willingly were highly inconvenienced, in some cases with inclement weather, a lack of adequate parking, masses having to walk great distances, young and old, only to stand, some for hours with no seating available.

Why did they do it? Because of passion. They had a passion to see change. They wanted to send a message to our government and specifically to our president that they didn't like him or his leadership style. Again, they were motivated by passion. My question is this: *What if there were thousands who would come together in every city across the USA, willing to be greatly inconvenienced because they were so convinced that prayer would produce the greatest change our nation would ever see?*

Coming together...

- Not because of who's speaking. No well-known musicians or bands.
- Willing to walk great distances because of a lack of convenient parking.
- Willing to stand for possible hours, no matter the weather.
- All willing to be inconvenienced because of passion.
- Passion for the presence of the King of kings.

We all want to see change. Protesting has the potential to change *who* is the leader. But prayer has the power to change the *heart* of the leader. I am convinced that between the two, prayer has greater power to bring more significant transformation than protest. Protest gets the attention of humanity.

Prayer gets the attention of heaven. One encounter with Jesus resulted in this question: "Did not our hearts burn within us?" Passion in our hearts will result in desperation for the presence of Jesus. Desperation for Jesus comes out of humility in character. Humility in character will result in unity in mission. Unity in mission will result in healing in our nation. There is no inconvenience in passion.

Prayer from a Higher Perspective

Can you believe it? Drones? Who would have thought there would be a time when so many would be so anxious about such a thing? There are two things that cause many to be concerned, and even fearful, about the recent sightings of drones of unknown origin:

- they potentially offer surveillance from a higher perspective,
- they potentially can carry weapons.

But did you know that the same could be said for effective prayer? I know that this might be a stretch, but there is a parallel between the two. I have a friend that does YouTube videos of his excursions on the beautiful lake regions in Canada. I am fascinated when he is taking footage of the surrounding areas from a drone, a thousand feet in the air. It is stunning.

If you have ever seen mountains from a higher perspective, they don't look as impossible to cross as they do when you are at ground level. So, when you pray, see the answer from above – from a thousand feet above your trouble – and you will be encouraged, lifted up. When we pray, we get to see the answers to our prayers coming from a higher perspective. From heaven's point of view, God sees you and He sees your need.

If we believe God's promises, Jesus said: "When you pray, you can say to this mountain, 'Be removed and cast into the sea,' and it will happen." What are the mountains He is talking about? Anything that is standing in the way between you and God's plans for your "hope and future." Oh, and the weapons?

The greatest, most effective, and most powerful weapon available to us is—**prayer.**

> *"We are human, but we don't wage war as humans do. We use God's mighty weapons, not worldly weapons, to knock down the strongholds of human reasoning and to destroy [lies of deception]. We destroy every proud obstacle that keeps people from knowing God. We capture their rebellious thoughts and teach them to follow Christ."* (2 Corinthians 10:3–5)

Worship of Jesus will demolish worry and fear. So today, you can "cast your care on Him, for He cares for you." (See 1 Peter 5:7)

SEEKING, TRUSTING, AND COMING HOME

CHAPTER 12

I have a friend who was given the responsibility to watch his young grandson at the Minnesota State Fair. He told me later that he was distracted for just a few moments when he realized that he had lost track of the little boy in the massive crowd. Fear seized him and increased with every beat of his heart. He jumped up on a bench and just started screaming his grandson's name. He didn't care what anyone would think. The only thing he had in mind—he was consumed only with finding this child that he deeply loved.

He ran in circles, panic-stricken, constantly calling his name. And then... there he was, standing all alone, confused but calm. He heard his grandpa's voice and knew that he wasn't alone. He was found. However, the trauma of this event would be etched into my friend's mind.

You know, there is a difference between the two words:

- **Seeking** and
- **Travailing.**

Seeking is what you do when you lose your cell phone. Travailing is what you do when you lose your child. We have a promise that when we seek the Lord, we will find Him.

> *"In his pride the wicked man does not seek him; in all his thoughts there is no room for God."*(Psalm 10:4)

How do you seek God? By recognizing how helpless and hopeless you are without Him. When we don't have seeking the Lord as a priority, it is an indicator of undetected pride.

> *"The fool says in his heart, 'There is no God'... The Lord looks down from heaven on all mankind to see if there are any who understand, any who seek God."* (Psalm 14:1–2)

The greatest fool is the one who believes that there is a God but does not seek Him. Humility is at the core of seeking God, with a desire for intimacy with Him. "**I want to know Christ.**" Travailing is different. It is at the heart of intercession for our sons and daughters who need to come back home. And this is at the heart of a son who recognizes how lost he is and is crying out with longing and desperation for God to come and find him and forgive him. Jesus is seeking and travailing for you.

"Where Are You, God?"

If you are a living human being, you have had this question in your mind at one time or another. One thing that is common to everyone is that we all have experienced some level of disappointment in life. We prayed in the middle of our struggle and pain, and it seemed that God didn't answer. Disappointment because of unanswered prayer for your children, for your family, for healing from your affliction, and so on.

It's at that point that we have some options. We can blame ourselves. We can blame God. Or we just bury ourselves in addictions or activity. We either make "faith statements" because we are rightly conditioned to do so, or we become agnostic about the existence of God and even upset with those who make "faith statements," thinking that they aren't facing the world with reality. But deep down, we still ask—"God, where are You? Why didn't You answer? Why did You leave me alone in my heartache?" We ask because in the aching of our heart, we still do believe in the *existence* of God, but we question the **presence** of God. The resolution to this dilemma is simple and profound:

> *"'Seek me and you will find me when you seek me with all your heart. I will be found by you,' declares the Lord, 'and I will bring you back from your captivity...'"* (Jeremiah 29:13)

This might seem too simplistic to those who are struggling with faith right now. But the truth is disappointment, discouragement, and despair all seem assigned to hold you in captivity: captivity to separate you from the One who wants you to know the reality of His love. And the very thing that will set you free is the very presence of our Father in heaven – Himself. This takes something called *trust.* When you don't understand where He is, or why things didn't turn out the way you thought, that is the time trust will take you from the confinement of despair and bring you into the freedom of hope. Know this—in the center of your brokenness: "Standing somewhere in the shadows, you will find Him. You will know Him by the nail scars in His hands."

Time to Come Back

It is no wonder why there are those who have drifted away from having faith in God. It seems that the values and culture of the world are changing rapidly. There is such a strong pull on all of us to slowly and incrementally drift towards the reasoning of our culture that pervades every aspect of our lives – education, government, science, business, entertainment, and more. Human logic that excludes God is vulnerable to deception. And for deception to be effective it is undetectable. In other words, we aren't even aware of how far we are away from Jesus – or even care. Yes, it is no wonder that you might have lost your heart for God. Speaking of our day, Jesus said:

> *"Then many will stop following me and fall away, and they will betray one another and hate one another. And many [who are] lying will arise, deceiving multitudes*

> *and leading them away from the path of truth. There will be such an increase of the sin of lawlessness that those whose hearts once burned with passion for God and others will grow cold. But you, hold your hope firmly to the end and you will experience life and deliverance."* (Matthew 24:10–13, TPT)

Notice the solution to this cultural slide: "Hold your hope firmly to the end and you will experience life and deliverance." We must be intentional with holding on to our faith in Christ, and we must not let go. Be aware of what is influencing your ideas, concepts, philosophies, and thinking. Ask yourself:

- "Where is this current trend in thinking going to take us?"
- "What will it ultimately produce?"
- "What is the end result of my life and those around me if we continue in this direction?"

Conforming to the world around you happens incrementally. Transformation to the Lord happens intentionally. So, if you have drifted away from your faith in God—it is time to come back. He has never drifted from loving you.

> *"So, we tenderly plead with you on Christ's behalf, 'Turn back to God and be reconciled to him.'"* (2 Corinthians 5:20, TPT)

Come Back to Church

My life started in church. Sometimes I wonder if I was born in a pew. From my earliest memories, I remember how it seemed that every Sunday meeting was like a family reunion. It was our lifestyle. The first song I would ever learn was: "Jesus loves me, this I know." Really, it was wonderful. With all its problems and issues (and wherever there are humans, there are issues) there has been nothing like growing up in that kind of environment. I would still love to be in a room where the only music comes from the voices of a congregation of men and women lifted up in singing a hymn of worship, often augmented by an upright piano.

Even now, at this moment, I think of the hymn "Leaning On The Everlasting Arms,"[1] followed by the chorus, "Oh How I Love Jesus… [2]because He first loved me." Many times, when singing, I remember seeing tears in the eyes of men with their heads tilted towards heaven. What a great memory. The problem is, there are so many in this next generation who will not have that kind of recall. Too many are choosing not to give the first day of the week to gathering together to worship. As a result, many are missing out on the very core of what makes life complete: worshiping the Creator.

The truth is we all are made to function by our Creator, and we are all dysfunctional without Him. We don't realize it until a crisis comes and we then "come to our senses," with an awareness of our great need. It is when we recognize that we can't live without Him, we turn to Him—and He forgives us, accepts us, heals us, and leads us into growing into our purpose and reason for existence. The dysfunctional becomes functional.

Real church is a place constructed and established by God to provide a life-giving, hope-filled, loving, grace-filled environment, designed to encourage us to live life wisely and to direct the focus of our lives on Jesus. It is in this that we find our hope and will fulfill our reason for living.

Isn't it time for you to come back to church?

SECURE IN LOVE, STANDING IN HOPE

CHAPTER 13

What does a secure person look like in practice? Their life is marked by a tangible and radical love, evidenced by these distinctive qualities:

- They do not dishonor others but make them feel valuable.
- They don't demand their own way and are not stubborn.
- They are patient and kind.
- They are not jealous of others.
- Not boastful or proud, but humble.
- Not rude to others.
- They are not irritable or hateful.
- They are not self-promoting, but willing to be hidden.
- *Not easily angered or bitter.*

- They keep no record of wrongs and admit when they are wrong.
- They are forgiving and merciful.
- They are willing to be vulnerable.
- They have no pleasure in injustice.
- They possess integrity and are elated when truth wins.
- They always protect.
- They always trust.
- *They never give up.*
- They never lose faith.
- They are always hopeful.
- They endure through every circumstance.

Those who are secure ultimately will not fail—because they know how to love. And *love never fails*. (See 1 Corinthians 13:4–7.) I pray that you are saturated with the powerful, everlasting love of God today.

Love, Hope, and the Groundwork of Miracles

Without realizing the extent of God's love, we lack an expectation that He will fulfill His promises. We put them off to "someday" instead of "today." But expectant hope is the groundwork—it is the foundation for miracles and healing. That hope comes from knowing that God's love is perfect and complete—fully focused on you.

When it seems that He hasn't answered our cry for help, we tend to develop a reliance on our own understanding. Then we interpret His will according to our circumstances instead of relying on His promises. When we don't understand what God is doing, we tend to default to our own reasoning—and find ourselves wandering—without hope, without faith, and without love. That is why—and that is when—we must *intentionally choose to trust in Him.*

Trust in His promises,

- Trust in His presence,
- Especially when you don't understand—trust His love.

Trusting God, when you don't understand God, creates within you a capacity for increase in your love for Him. It affirms your heart's desire. The more you **trust**, the more you long for His presence and the fulfillment of His promise. When your hope is "deferred,"—you *keep on hoping*. It really isn't my love for Him, but His love for me, and the expectation that He hasn't forgotten me, that gives me hope when things seem hopeless. Hearing this again causes faith to arise.

It all starts with love

"Without faith it is impossible to please God."[1]
and *without hope* it is impossible to have faith.
and without love it is impossible to have hope.
When love increases—hope increases.
When hope increases—faith increases.
"The greatest of these is love."[2]

Fear Not!

For many, the *fear of the future* is more real than hope for the future. We have so much information and disinformation funneling into us—forming us. And it seems that the more information we have, the more we struggle with fear and unbelief. But remember—every time the angels appeared in the Christmas story, the first thing they said was: "Do not be afraid."

To Zechariah,
To Mary,
To Joseph,
To the shepherds.

The angel's proclamation always began with these words:"Do not be afraid." They came with something more than just information. They brought revelation. A revelation of the glory, the heart, and the love of God for His creation and for all of humanity, which includes you.

- Sometimes too much information can cause a *hard heart*—But revelation of the glory of God results in a yielded heart.
- Sometimes too much information can cause pride—But revelation of the glory of God results in *humility*.
- Sometimes too much information can keep our focus on darkness—But revelation of the glory of God results in knowing His presence.

Often, *information* comes from researching. But revelation comes through searching—for the glory of the Father. What is the glory? It is the tangible nearness of

God that becomes so real, even those who don't believe—begin to believe. So, the message for us is: do not be afraid of what the future holds. Trust in the One who holds the future, and His glory will surround you today.

> *"What, then, shall we say in response to these things? If God is for us, who can be against us? He who did not spare his own Son, but gave him up for us all—how will he not also, along with him, graciously give us all things?"* (Romans 8:31–32, NIV)

> *"...For He has said, 'I will never [under any circumstances] desert you [nor give you up nor leave you without support, nor will I in any degree leave you helpless], nor will I forsake or let you down or relax My hold on you [assuredly not]!' So we take comfort and are encouraged and confidently say, 'The Lord is my helper [in time of need], I will not be afraid.'"* (Hebrews 13:5–6, AMP)

> *"With long life I will satisfy him and show him my salvation."* (Psalm 91:16, NIV)

> I receive this promise today.

> *"Teach us to number our days, that we may gain a heart of wisdom."* (Psalm 90:12, NIV)

We all have an expiration date. When you realize how short life is compared to eternity, you begin to make *quality decisions* within your days. This is called wisdom!

(see *Psalm 90:12 (NIV)* What causes a person to risk everything in their life to save another? The answer might surprise you. Many would say courage. However, I believe the answer is *passion.* It's passion that turns a job into joy, And duty into desire. It changes the heart of a servant into a son, And the heart of a son into a servant. You cannot separate passion from suffering.

"IF YOU HAVE NOTHING IN LIFE TO DIE FOR, YOU HAVE NOTHING IN LIFE TO LIVE FOR."

For what you love in life, you will give everything. (So be careful what captures your heart.) When you are moved with passion, suffering becomes insignificant. With the motivation of compassion, you will endure anything. A passionate person will do what a passive person would not do. Passionate people will lay down their life. The cause is their priority. Passive people just want to lay down. Convenience and comfort is their priority.

Passion Week began with Jesus riding into Jerusalem in triumph. But at the end of the week, there is a startling contrast. On Friday, He hung on a cross, suffering and broken, in what looked like defeat. Jesus faced this week because of His passion for those who were broken and hurting—people like you and me.

Oh, how *we need passion* again. Without passion, vision perishes. Passion is the fuel of mission and purpose. I am so thankful that someone had passion for me. They showed me the burning love of Jesus. As a result: "I once was lost but now I am found." Jesus wasn't just performing a function or fulfilling a mission—He was, and is, filled with **love** and passion. He went to the cross because of His deep desire and longing for you. He carefully placed one stone upon another. He designed, carved, and shaped the timbers that would hold it in place. It was crude to be sure.

And yet, even with the few and inadequate tools and materials available, as he stood back and looked at the finished structure, as simple as it was, he knew that it would be enough to accomplish his purposes. All he had left to do was build a manger. You see, **he had a dream**. One day he would have some sheep, he would own some cattle, and even a donkey that would need protection from the harsh elements of winter. But little did he know that one day, that simply put together stable would be the place where:

- Darkness would be filled with light,
- Despair would be turned to hope,
- Hope would meet fear,
- Fear would encounter love,
- Failure would be conquered by forgiveness, and
- The Son of God would become the Savior of the world—and be laid in that very manger.

Little did he even consider what would happen in this humble, seemingly insignificant place. It would attract the attention of all of humanity. Wise men, farmers, shepherds, and all. If he would have only known—he might have done a better job. It is amazing what God can do *with just a stable.* It is amazing what God is going to do —*with you.*

An elderly man was slowly making his way towards me, leaning on his cane with every step. As he was about to pass by, I noticed that the insignia on his hat revealed that he was a veteran of the Chosin Reservoir battle in the Korean War. Not too long before, I had just read about the extreme hardship and loss of many lives our troops suffered in that terrible ordeal. So, I stopped and said, "Sir, thank you for your sacrifice in that awful conflict. I know that it was so hard." I will never forget the distant look in his eyes as he deliberately turned to me and asked, "Were you there?"

"No," I responded. "I only read about it in history."

He turned[3] away from me as he continued his walk. I heard him quietly say, "Yes, it was." "Were you there?"

There is an old hymn we would sing on Easter Sunday morning by that title: "Were you there when they nailed Him to a tree?—Oh, sometimes it causes me to tremble, tremble, tremble." And then the final verse was sung with great joy: "Were you there, when He rose up from the grave?"[4] Of course, the answer is no—I wasn't there. But I read about it. I read how *Jesus suffered on the cross* for all my faults and failures. He was beaten and bruised for all my sins, and I read that He took all my shame and brokenness upon Himself and died so that I – and you – could have forgiveness, mercy, grace, and eternal life.

I also read how on "the third day" after, He rose up alive and now lives forevermore. But it goes far beyond just reading about it. For me, and for millions and millions of others who have *encountered the love* of the risen Savior, it is an experience that brought the reality of the resurrection into our lives. You see, like many others: "I once was lost but now I am found." I once was spiritually dead, but because of the risen Christ, I am now alive. In Him, we are made new.

He changes despair into hope, addiction into freedom, hurting into healing, bitterness into forgiveness, brokenness into wholeness, and sinners into sons. And He is here. "Because He lives, I can face tomorrow."[5] Sometimes it causes me to shout:

Hallelujah!

ALWAYS CHOOSE LOVE

CHAPTER 14

"*Above all, clothe yourselves with love, which binds us all together in perfect harmony.*" (Colossians 3:14, NLT)

In a moment that stunned the sports world, Damar Hamlin, a safety for the Buffalo Bills, collapsed on the field after suffering cardiac arrest during a game against the Cincinnati Bengals. What happened next was nothing short of miraculous—and deeply moving. As medics rushed to his side, the entire stadium fell into a hush, and then, something powerful happened: People began to pray. Not just in the stands. Not just fans. Even the on-air sports analysts bowed their heads and lifted their voices to God, live on national television. In a rare moment of unity, the nation came together to CHOOSE LOVE through intercession and faith. And God intervened.

Damar Hamlin *lived*. He didn't just survive—he returned to the field as a starting safety for the Bills. On

September 23, 2022, he recorded his first career interception and led the team in defensive snaps. A man once dead—now fully alive and thriving. A true resurrection story in its own right. On his helmet, he wore the words:"CHOOSE LOVE." More than a slogan—it's a kingdom principle. And it's exactly what Jesus calls us to do.

Love Is Not a Feeling. It's a Choice.

In that same NFL season, "Choose Love" emerged as a theme even at the Super Bowl. But choosing love goes deeper than branding. It's more than a cultural moment. It's a daily decision. Many believe that people simply "fall" in love. While we may stumble into romance or attraction, real love—the kind that endures hardship, forgives enemies, and chooses peace—is never accidental. Love must be chosen. Intentionally. Repeatedly. Courageously. Jesus never said love would be easy. In fact, He warned us that a time would come when love would grow cold in many:

> "And because lawlessness will be increased, the love of many will grow cold. But the one who endures to the end will be saved." (Matthew 24:12–13, ESV)

Hate Is Easy. Love Requires Strength. Hate is natural. Love is supernatural. No one needs to be taught how to hate—it's often our default when we feel threatened, disrespected, or opposed. Hate arises when we let our emotions control our response, and when pride takes the wheel. But Scripture warns us of the danger in that path:

> *"Watch out that no poisonous root of bitterness grows up to trouble you, corrupting many." (Hebrews 12:15, NLT)*

Bitterness blinds us. Anger deceives us. When we are easily offended, frequently bitter, and resistant to truth, we've likely been deceived—just as Jesus warned:

> *"Watch out that no one deceives you... For many will turn away from Me... and betray and hate each other...Sin will be rampant everywhere, and the love of many will grow cold." (Matthew 24:4,10, 12 NLT)*

Love is the True Test of Truth

If you want to know whether you're walking in truth or deception, examine your capacity to love—especially when it's hard. Those who walk in truth will display the fruit of the Spirit:

> *"love, joy, peace, patience, kindness, goodness, faithfulness, gentleness, and self-control."* (Galatians 5:22–23)

But when deception takes hold, we begin to resist love, and instead become reactionary, bitter, and hardened.

> *"By this everyone will know that you are My disciples, if you love one another." (John 13:35)*

Choose Love. Choose Jesus.

To love your enemies. To forgive those who hurt you. To speak truth with grace. These are not passive actions; they are powerful choices—decisions made by hearts that are led by the Holy Spirit. Each time you choose love, you strengthen your heart to endure. You resist the drift of the world and align yourself with the Kingdom of God.

"Do not be overcome by evil, but overcome evil with good." *(Romans 12:21)*

Even when it's unpopular. Even when it's hard. Even when you're misunderstood...

Choose Love.

Choose Truth.

Choose Jesus.

Because when you do, you're not just choosing to feel better—you're choosing to WIN.

HOPE FOR MINNESOTA

CHAPTER 15

I care deeply about Minnesota. Like many of you, I've asked the question that weighs heavily on hearts across our state: *"Who's going to fix our broken state?"* Right now, hope feels scarce for so many. As I served as Senate Chaplain for years, I often spoke to our legislators about hope for Minnesota. I shared my conviction that a day is coming when the nation will look at us and say, "*Now that's the way government should function.*"

I know—especially in this season—that sounds almost impossible. To many, our present condition looks like the opposite of that vision. Yet I still believe God has a plan—for our state, and for our cities. In spite of the brokenness, the apparent sins, and the derision some in the nation direct toward us, I have not changed my perspective. I remain convinced there is hope. I still declare that Minnesota will be known as a place of healing and restoration.

For this to become reality, we must embrace repentance for the past sins we have committed against one another and against God. We must make a quality decision—moment by moment—to forgive each other, even to love our enemies. Instead of canceling them, we will love our enemies and choose to care about them.

- When even our leaders lack integrity, we will embrace honesty.
- When dignity is absent, we will choose honor.
- When people are arrogant, we will embrace humility.
- When compassion fades, we will extend love—even to those who oppose us.

In short, for this to be possible, we desperately need Jesus. We need His love for the world—not a love for systems or ideologies, but His passion for flawed, imperfect people—just like you and me. Because of that love, He went to the cross for sinners like us.

Therefore, as Colossians urges us:

> *"...Clothe yourselves with compassion, kindness, humility, gentleness and patience... And over all these virtues put on love, which binds them all together in perfect unity. Let the peace of Christ rule in your hearts, since as members of one body you were called to peace. And be thankful."*
> (Colossians 3:12, 14–15, NIV)

We can enter into judgment filled with anger, or we can cry out to God for mercy. Let's choose the latter.

As I write these words, my own heart is swirling with emotion. I feel a deep heaviness—a genuine brokenness—for the masses who are enraged, exhausted, frustrated, chaotic, and confused. Yes, I feel anger too. But my anger is not aimed at people. I am grieved that an open door has allowed **"the thief [to] come only to steal and kill and destroy"** (John 10:10).

I am angry at the spiritual darkness that seems, for the moment, to be prevailing. Yet even here, I carry an enduring, unshakable hope. As I weep for our state and our nation, I remain confident: *this will turn around*. God has not abandoned us. His light will break through.

Resist Emotional and Political Reactivity

In this hour, we must resist reacting emotionally or politically. We cannot afford to accept everything we see on social media or hear in the news. Too much deception is fueling confusion and even anarchy. God calls us higher:

> *"Above all else, guard your heart, for everything you do flows from it."* (Proverbs 4:23)

A Promise for Dark Times

This morning, my heart was drawn to Isaiah's promise:

> *"Arise, shine, for your light has come, and the glory of the LORD rises upon you. See, darkness covers the earth and thick darkness is over the peoples, but the LORD rises*

upon you and his glory appears over you. Nations will come to your light..." (Isaiah 60:1–3)

Though it was written to Israel, I sensed the Lord asking, "Could this also be My heart for Minnesota?" Even when thick darkness seems to cover our cities, I believe the narrative over the Twin Cities will change.

A New Identity Over Minnesota

It is time for a shift in our identity. Our current struggles will not define our future. Minnesota will still be called Minnesota—derived from the Dakota words meaning "the land where the water reflects the skies." But I believe God is declaring a prophetic future: "Minnesota—the land where the people reflect My glory."

When the nation speaks of us, it will no longer be with contempt, but with admiration. Many will come to our light.

Do Not Fight Darkness With Darkness

We must refuse to overcome evil with more evil. Instead,

> *"Do not be overcome by evil, but overcome evil with good."* (Romans 12:21)

The world may see us today as a state in chaos, but we will not let present circumstances dictate our destiny. We are called to be a Revival State—a people of light, a people of hope, a people who reflect the glory of God. So, let's intentionally agree with God's design. Don't give up. Don't give in. Refuse to agree with the darkness. Agree with God's heart. God gives us a promise of restoration:

> *"Then you shall call, and the LORD will answer; you shall cry, and he will say, 'Here I am.'"* (Isaiah 58:9a, ESV)
>
> *"Your ancient ruins shall be rebuilt; you shall raise up the foundations of many generations; you shall be called the Repairer of the Breach, the Restorer of Streets to Dwell In."* (Isaiah 58:12, ESV)

This is God's vision for us.

The Spirit Is Hovering Again

Remember the beginning:

> *"The earth was without form and void, and darkness was over the face of the deep... And the Spirit of God was hovering over the face of the waters."* (Genesis 1:2)

Darkness is never the end of the story. It is simply the canvas on which God declares, "Let there be light!" So today, with faith and expectation, we pray together:

Come, Holy Spirit! Come with your glorious Light!

THE TESTIMONY OF TOWDAH

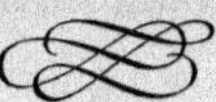

CHAPTER 16

A Shout of Love

We have walked together through a lot in these pages. We've talked about division and healing, anger and forgiveness, hate and love, protest and prayer, judgment and mercy. We've looked at cities, nations, families, and hearts that are broken—and we've heard Jesus calling us to be peacemakers, to "break the cycle," and to choose love when everything around us is choosing something else.

As we come to the end of this book, I want to leave you with one more picture:

A people walking around impossible walls

Silent.

Waiting.

Then lifting up a shout of praise that brings those walls down. The Bible calls this kind of praise a sacrifice of thanksgiving. In Hebrew, it is called Towdah. There's a unique joy in being part of the family of God—a connection that unites us in the profound love we share for Jesus. No matter our differences, we are bound together in purpose, worship, and faith. And one of the most powerful ways we "choose love" is by choosing thanksgiving over complaint, praise over fear, and worship over worry. The first generation of Israelites coming out of Egypt fell into a pattern of criticism, complaint, and unbelief. It kept them out of the Promised Land.

JOSHUA'S GENERATION WAS CALLED TO LIVE DIFFERENTLY.

God told them:

- March around Jericho once a day for six days.
- Say nothing. Not one word.
- On the seventh day, march seven times—then shout.

That silence was not empty. It was a reset. God was retraining their hearts. No more agreeing with fear. No more rehearsing all the reasons it "won't work." No more magnifying the size of the walls instead of the size of their God. Then came the shout. It wasn't just noise. It was Towdah – thanksgiving *before* the breakthrough, praise *before* the walls fell, faith *before* the answer could be seen. And God responded.

In our day, we have our own Jerichos:

- Walls of division between political groups, races, and communities.
- Walls of pain in marriages, families, and friendships.
- Walls of fear, anxiety, addiction, and despair.

The easy thing is to complain, criticize, and accuse. But we are not called to live the "easy thing." We are called to live the Jesus way. We are called to:

- Love when others hate.
- Forgive when others stay bitter.
- Bless when others curse.
- Pray when others only protest.
- Give thanks when others only grumble.

This is what Towdah looks like in our time:

> "*Even though the fig trees have no blossoms, and there are no grapes on the vines... yet I will rejoice in the Lord! I will be joyful in the God of my salvation.*" (Habakkuk 3:17–18, NLT)

It is choosing to say: "Thank You, Lord," not because everything is perfect, but because He is faithful, and we trust Him in the middle of the imperfection. I have seen this in my own life. There have been moments when I made mistakes that could have caused real damage—times I could have easily slipped into fear, shame, and self-condemnation. But instead, in those moments, I have chosen to stop, lift my hands, and say: "Thank You, Lord.

I trust You to turn this around." And again and again, He has. Not because I got everything right. But because He is good.

Towdah doesn't pretend the problem isn't real. Towdah invites God into the middle of it. So, as we close this book, let me ask you:

- What are the walls in your life?
- Where have you been tempted to complain instead of praise?
- Where have you chosen anger instead of love, accusation instead of mercy, fear instead of faith?

TODAY, YOU CAN MAKE A DIFFERENT CHOICE.

You can:

- Choose love instead of hate.
- Choose forgiveness instead of bitterness.
- Choose blessing instead of cursing.
- Choose prayer instead of despair.
- Choose thanksgiving instead of complaint.

You can lift up a shout of praise over your family, your city, your nation, and your own heart—even before you see the change.

> "*Come before His presence with thanksgiving; let us shout joyfully to Him with psalms.*" (Psalm 95:2)

Shout—not because everything looks good—but because God is good. If you've never fully surrendered your life to Jesus, this is your moment. You don't have to fix yourself first. You don't have to have all the answers. You simply come. Pray from your heart:

> "Lord Jesus, I believe You love me. I repent of my sins and ask You to be my Savior and Lord. Thank You for forgiving me, for giving me a new heart, and a new life. Teach me to love like You love. Amen."

Welcome to the family of God! Now, join the rest of us—weak, imperfect, forgiven people—who are learning, day by day, to choose love. So here, at the end of this book, I invite you to stand—in your living room, in your kitchen, in your church, wherever you are—and with a thankful heart, declare over your life, your family, your city, and your nation:

"Jesus, I choose love. I choose forgiveness. I choose mercy. I choose praise. I trust You. Bring the walls down."

Because in the end, the greatest force on earth is not hate. It is not anger. It is not fear. It is God's everlasting love.

"I have loved you with an everlasting love..." (Jeremiah 31:3, ESV)—a love that nothing can separate us from (Romans 8:38–39, ESV).

Praise God, from whom all blessings flow—whose love never fails, and whose mercy knows no end.

EPILOGUE

A DEFINING MOMENT

In light of the day we are living in, I'm reminded of the question posed by Francis A. Schaeffer: "How then should we live?"[1] It's a question that presses on all of us. *What can I do to make a difference?*

I believe—deeply—that you and I can, and will, see lasting, transformational change. But that change will not come by accident. It begins when we are intentional about guarding our own hearts from the external pressure to conform to the spirit of the culture around us. When we resist that pressure and choose God's way instead, it produces real and enduring fruit.

Isaiah 58:9 (TPT) says: "*If you banish every form of oppression, the scornful accusations, and vicious slander...*"

I sense God speaking clearly to us in this moment: *Demonstrate My love by giving and serving others. You are not called to be an accuser—but an encourager. (see* 1 Thessalonians 5:11; 1 John 3:18)

Resist being defined as one who tears down, and

instead be known as one who builds up. The quality decisions we make to follow God's heart in these matters will determine the outcome. They shape more than our actions—they define our identity. And ultimately, they determine our destiny.

> *"Then you shall call, and the LORD will answer; you shall cry, and he will say, 'Here I am...'" (Isaiah 58:9a, ESV)*
>
> *"And your ancient ruins shall be rebuilt; you shall raise up the foundations of many generations; you shall be called the repairer of the breach, the restorer of streets to dwell in." Isaiah 58:12, ESV)*

This is our defining moment—to show the world our true identity in Christ, for Jesus said, *"By this everyone will know that you are My disciples, if you love one another."*

Choose love.

ENDNOTES

1. THE 'PRESENCE' STATE

1. Paraphrase of 1 Corinthians 11:28, 31
2. Romans 8:14 (NIV).
3. John 7:24 (NIV).
4. A Precarious State: A Documentary for Minnesota's Future, produced by Kupchella Public Affairs, LLC, first aired October 2, 2025, available at PreciousState.com and on YouTube.
5. (Isaiah 58:12, NKJV/MSG).
6. Random House Unabridged Dictionary, s.v. "foundation," via Infoplease.com / WordReference.com.

2. THANKSGIVING, BLESSING, AND THE ATMOSPHERE AROUND US

1. [1]Elvina M. Hall, *"Jesus Paid It All"* (1865), public domain.

3. PEACEMAKERS IN A CULTURE OF CONFLICT

1. 1 Corinthians 13:4–7 (paraphrased)

6. SONS, DAUGHTERS, AND THE FATHER'S LOVE

1. (Matthew 16:18, ESV)

7. CITIES, NATIONS, AND THE PRESENCE OF GOD

1. [hope] has been added as a devotional amplification of the text.

8. KINGS, KINGDOMS, AND HUMILITY

1. Noah Webster, *American Dictionary of the English Language* (1828), s.v. "king.
2. Early church sources such as Irenaeus and Jerome describe Polycarp as having been instructed by the Apostle John, which is why he's traditionally counted among the Apostolic Fathers. See *Polycarp*, Wikipedia, accessed January 20, 2026, https://en.wikipedia.org/wiki/Polycarp.
3. *The Martyrdom of Polycarp*, early 2nd century. https://www.newadvent.org/fathers/0102.htm.
4. (Scripture paraphrased from 2 Chronicles 7:14. Emphasis added.)

9. JUSTICE, MERCY, AND THE VALUE OF LIFE

1. **United States Declaration of Independence**, preamble (1776).

10. FORGIVENESS, GENERATIONS, AND HEALING

1. The phrase "the great king" is an explanatory addition to the text.

12. SEEKING, TRUSTING, AND COMING HOME

1. *Leaning on the Everlasting Arms*, hymn composed by Anthony J. Showalter with lyrics by Showalter and Elisha A. Hoffman, published 1887; inspired by *Deuteronomy* 33:27.
2. Frederick Whitfield, *O How I Love Jesus*, c. 1855. Public domain. Accessed January 20, 2026. https://hymnary.org/text/there_is_a_name_i_love_-to_hear_i_love.

13. SECURE IN LOVE, STANDING IN HOPE

1. Hebrews 11:6
2. 1 Corinthians 13:13

3. Lines from the traditional African-American spiritual “Were You There?” (Public Domain).
4. Footnote 1: Lines from the traditional African-American spiritual “Were You There?” (Public Domain).
5. *Because He Lives”*, Bill & Gloria Gaither (1971)

17. EPILOGUE

1. Francis A. Schaeffer, *How Should We Then Live?* (Wheaton, IL: Crossway Books, 1976)

ACKNOWLEDGMENTS

I am profoundly thankful for my family, my greatest blessing. They have made me feel like the wealthiest man alive. Truly, "Children are God's love-gift; they are heaven's generous reward. Happy will be the couple who has many of them...for your offspring will have influence and honor to prevail on your behalf!" (Psalm 127:3, 5, TPT).

My deep gratitude extends to the staff and congregation of Redeeming Love Church. For nearly 45 years, we have been partners in serving Jesus. You have faithfully embraced the vision to focus not just on church growth, but on changing a city. As a result, we have grown together, sharing a significant and common calling.

I am also grateful for all the pastors, government, and business leaders with whom I have had the privilege of serving in mission over the years. I am always reminded that there is only one church, and we are all one "staff" together. To the mentors who invested in my life, thank you. All of your lives have made a lasting difference. We have only just begun!

A special thank you to Yolandita Colón, who spent many long hours compiling and editing this work. She has been a spiritual daughter for whom I am so thankful. She, along with Sandi, continually inspired and encouraged me to bring this project to completion, believing it would give hope to many. From time to time, people have asked if I would put these posts into a book. Well, with thanks to Yolandita who took the step further, here it is.

This book is a compilation of posts from recent years. The title captures the core message of what I believe is the most powerful force for deep, profound change in our culture: to **Choose Love**. This means living intentionally to bring the reality of God's presence into our cities and nation. I believe it is our only hope for true transformation.

This vision is beautifully expressed in Isaiah 58:10-12 (TPT): "*And if you offer yourselves in compassion for the hungry and relieve those in misery, then your dawning light will rise in the darkness and your gloom will turn into noonday splendor! YAHWEH will always guide you where to go and what to do. He will fill you with refreshment even when you are in a dry, difficult place. He will continually restore strength to you, so you will flourish like a well-watered garden and like an ever-flowing, trustworthy spring of blessing. Your people will rebuild long-deserted ruins, building anew on foundations laid long before you. You will be known as Repairers of the Cities and Restorers of Communities.*"

It is to this holy work of restoration that we are called.

ABOUT THE AUTHOR

Rev. Michael D. Smith—known to most simply as Pastor Mike—has served as a pastor and spiritual leader in the Twin Cities of Minnesota for more than four decades. In 1981, God placed a defining vision in his heart—not just to pastor a church, but to pastor a city. That calling has shaped every season of his ministry and continues to guide his leadership today.

In 1993, this vision led Pastor Mike and the congregation he served toward St. Paul. With a desire to be positioned closer to the urban center, the church was renamed Redeeming Love Church, and a building was purchased in Maplewood. From this place, Pastor Mike and his wife, Sandi, have faithfully served as Senior Pastors for nearly 45 years, investing deeply in the spiritual renewal of both St. Paul and Minneapolis.

For more than three decades, Pastor Mike and Redeeming Love Church have been committed to bringing the hope of the Gospel to the city—believing they are called to see atmospheres of despair, poverty, and brokenness transformed into atmospheres of hope, healing, and generosity, one life at a time. He carries a deep conviction that Saint Paul, with an apostolic destiny of influence, can become a model for the nation—an urban center once marked by brokenness becoming a revival epicenter of hope and healing.

Deeply committed to regional Kingdom partnership, Pastor Mike has helped connect pastors and churches across denominational and cultural backgrounds through initiatives such as St. Paul Pastors' Prayer, Prayer Transformation Ministries, Cities Church (St. Paul and Minneapolis pastors), the Minnesota Prophetic Conference, and the International Healing Conference. He is also one of three pastors who helped launch the St. Paul Mayor's Prayer Breakfast and has opened Redeeming Love Church to host significant citywide and statewide gatherings.

Beyond the church walls, Pastor Mike has served the wider community as Police Chaplain for White Bear Lake, as a chaplain to the Minnesota Senate, and for many years on the Executive Board of Minnesota Adult & Teen Challenge, where he is recognized as a founding board member, championing Christ-centered addiction recovery in Minnesota and beyond.

Married to his beloved wife, Sandi, for over 50 years,

Pastor Mike is a devoted husband, father, grandfather, and great-grandfather. Together they have three children, eight grandchildren, and two great-grandchildren who love and serve the Lord. His life and ministry reflect a multigenerational legacy of faith, grace, and devotion to Jesus Christ—values that continue to shape his leadership, teaching, and passion for cities and generations.

 instagram.com/msmith.rlc
 facebook.com/msmith.rlc

CALL TO ACTION

If this book encouraged you, we invite you to take one simple next step.

- **Leave an honest review on Amazon** to help others discover this message
- **Share this book with someone** who may need hope, clarity, or healing in divided times

Your voice helps extend the reach of this message far beyond one reader.

To stay connected and receive updates, resources, and future messages from Pastor Mike, visit:

PastorMikeSmith.net

Together, we can help carry this message of Christlike love to a world in need.

www.ingramcontent.com/pod-product-compliance
Lightning Source LLC
LaVergne TN
LVHW011047110826
845149LV00015B/3382

* 9 7 8 1 9 6 4 6 7 3 0 8 0 *